The *Girlz*

Run the World *in Pearls*

GUILDED JOURNAL FOR WRITING YOUR TESTIMONIAL TO UNVEIL YOUR MASK

By
Annette Watson-Johnson

THE GIRLZ RUN THE WORLD IN PEARLS

GUIDED JOURNAL FOR WRITING YOUR TESTIMONIAL TO UNVEIL YOUR MASK

Testimonials Introduced By
Annette Watson-Johnson

Girlz Run The World In Pearls

Journal For Writing Your Testimonial To Unveil Your Mask

Published in the United States of America

Annette Watson-Johnson

ISBN: 978-0-578-78030-6

Edited by

Jeffrey White, Yes We Did LLC
yeswedid@jwfitnesssolutions.com

Cover Illustration by
Hi-Def Media

Author's photographs by
Emage Studio

PERMISSION STATEMENTS FOR THE USE OF VARIOUS BIBLE VERSIONS

This Book is Presented to

_____

By

_____

For The Occasion Of

_____

Date

_____

Table of Contents

Dedication

This guided journal for writing your testimonial is created to encourage women from all over the world to begin a journey of healing. It is especially designed for those who have made mental, physical, and spiritual sacrifices for themselves, their families and communities. This journal is for those who suppressed their vision due to the disparities that created adversities and as a result have held them back but are now ready to unveil these masks of negative traditions.

Ladies grab your pearls and be prepared to join the **GIRLZ RUN THE WORLD IN PEARLS MOVEMENT!**

Annette's Acknowledgement

I want to thank God for entrusting me with this beautiful gift of prophetic dreams, entrepreneurship, and the vision to build platforms to help people get mentally, physically and spiritually well as he has instructed me to. I want to praise God for my parents Elder John & Addie Watson. They both help me to comprehend that God don't make mistakes and that my gifts are given to me and I am blessed for it. I thank my children Provine Cosby Jr. & Octavia Cosby for all they do to support me. Thanks to my husband Reginald E. Johnson for being my rock when I need him. Hats off to my 10 brothers and sisters (Jan, Norvell (deceased), Dana, John Jr., Clara, Benard, Hosanna, Marietta, Demetrius and Donnell) for believing in me and lending me their listening ears at all times of the day. My best friend Tammy Watkins and Goddaughter Tamala Watkins, and a huge shout out to my husband's side of the family for all of their support. To my cousin Antoinette (Toni) Brown, you are always willing and ready to assist when I need you.

Introduction

This guided journal for writing your testimonial will take you on a step by step process to create your own personal testimonial/s. In the paperback version you can write up to three testimonials. This journey will unveil the mask of negative traditions to encourage, heal, deliver, uplift, inspire, and reveal the jewel (pearl) in you. This journal for writing your testimonial works as a great resource for women all over the world. In addition, it will allow for incorporating my journaling techniques into schools, churches, prisons, youth organizations, families, or corporate settings, helping to unveil the mask of many underlying concerns.

In my journal you will be encouraged to reflect and record in detail everything from your feelings about a particular situation in your social life to your thoughts on a current event in the political world. This journal serves a wide range of purposes to include recording your testimonial just as the seven collaborating Authors did in my book "Girlz Run The World In Pearls – Unveiling The Mask To Reveal Our Pearls". Because of the breakthrough, deliverance, and successful feedback from the Authors and readers, I was encouraged to create this writing journal so that others could utilize the same writing process I used as a template in that book. The Authors had major revelations and wrote testimonials that had never been told before. Keep it private and share only when you are ready. So make sure you have your tissue for tears, and pens or pencils to begin your unveiling, then find a quite spot in your domicile. Let this guided journal for writing your testimonial aid you in discovering your inner survivor by embracing valuable power and strengths ultimately formed during times of adversity.

 Once you complete this guided journal for writing your testimonial grab your pearls and join the **GIRLZ RUN THE WORLD IN PEARLS MOVEMENT** by wearing your pearls as you badge of deliverance from your adversities. You will be delivered and ready to execute your dream and visions!

The Pearl

I am pulling this information as well and a few others from my book collaboration entitled "Girlz Run The World In Pearls Unveiling The Mask To Reveal Our Pearls" (pages 11-15) because it is relevant to understand the correlation between our adversities and the pearl. There are so many definitions for the word *"PEARL"* or *"Pearl.."*. It is also an acronym. Depending on the company or organization that utilizes it in this form, it usually represents a shortened name or mission. I am not a member of any sorority, but I know most of them wear pearls because they represent or symbolize something of importance. You are not privy to the why unless you pledge and get inducted into the sisterhood. We are excited to now have Mrs. Kamala Harris, a black woman be Vice President elect of the United States. Since she is a member of a sorority, we will see her wearing pearls on a regular basis. In reference to the contents of this book, we are defining the word "Pearl" as a *"jewel that symbolizes our exodus from the disparities that lead to our adversities."* Therefore, we women who have overcome adversities are jewels and should wear our pearls to represent them proudly.

I have noticed that there is a correlation between a natural pearl and the adversities that affect many women and girls from around the world. We are the victims of so many crimes against humanity. Depending on your race and continent, we are not seen as equal and our rights to fairness come into question more often than not. We hit more brick walls than men. If you are a black woman you can double the numbers.

We strive to do it all against the odds, but that sometimes can lead to adversities that hinder us from reaching our destiny in life. We all have a story, but the outcome is determined by what part of the world you live in. We all share a common denominator that consists of wanting what is best for us, our families, the community we live in and the sacrifices we will make to protect it. In most instances, pearls are formed under the same premise.

A natural pearl is formed organically when a foreign substance or irritant invades the oyster's soft tissue muscle (the mantle) intentionally or accidentally. The mantle is the oyster's internal organ. When the oysters eat, the mantle uses the minerals to produce the nacre which creates its shell. The foreign substance or irritant could occur from an attack (irritant) by another grain of sand, ocean creature, a parasite, or an injury.

Once the oyster encounters a foreign substance or irritant, it begins to repair itself in a kind of immune system-like way. It will cover the foreign substance or irritant with layers of nacre. This process usually creates the shell but will form a pearl instead. The natural pearl becomes a beautiful jewel formed in many colors as the result of this biological process. These freshwater pearls can take between 1 and 6 years to form, whereas saltwater pearls may take between 5 and 20 years. The longer a pearl stays in the shell buried in the bottom of the ocean, the more nacre forms and the larger the pearl.

Since the beginning of time, pearls have been known to be the ultimate symbols for wisdom. Valued for their calming effects, pearls represent serenity, while being able to strengthen valuable relationships and convey a sense of safety. Pearls also symbolize purity, as well as integrity and loyalty. Pearls represent wisdom gained through experience. The gems of the ocean are believed to offer protection to the wearer, as well as attract good luck and wealth. Moreover, pearls speak of the wearer's purity and integrity (thepearlsource.com).

Natural pearls are created in the ocean and quite rare. It can take more than 100,000 deep-ocean-living creatures to make just one strand of pearls, but oysters are the primary source of these natural pearls. They are mentioned in the Bible numerous times and were adorned by great kings & queens, often revered as status indicators. Today, they are rarer and more expensive than ever, often used in a less expensive, costume style fashion.

There are no outwardly visible signs that an oyster has a pearl inside. You just have to open it to see. But what we learned from an oyster is that it will sit in the bottom of the ocean and the pearl will continue to form inside of it. Like pearls, many of us have had irritants invade our being. We are also growing these pearls of wisdom but are keeping them hidden at the bottom of our ocean. Just like a fisherman will deep dive to discover these priceless jewels will we do the same? Those irritants could have been rape, abuse, hurt or any other negative tradition that caused us to be held back. The best way to release our pearls is by acknowledging what it is and how it affected you mentally, physically, and spiritually. If you don't it will continue to rob you of your vision.

One way to release is to testify: our testimonials relate to the blessings that we encounter as well as real life adversities we face in our daily lives. The church has been the forefront of using this method because it encourages the congregation to have faith and learn from other's experiences.

A testimony is powerful because it is a story about an exodus from an adversity or death-to-life experiences. Giving or hearing other's personal testimony is a way to provide comfort, unmask, shame the devil, share a deliverance, encourage, guide, or spread the gospel with others. This is accomplished by

explaining a personal salvation experience. It also gives others an example of how testimonials and God can change lives. It should be noted that many of our church testimonials leave out many details, such as who may have raped, beat, hurt, or stole, from us. This could be because many of our adversities have been a generational family tradition in which we have normalized. This may have been done to keep it all in the family to protect the family from shame or the irritant invader from falling into the hands of the biased justice system. With no voice or protection, we then continue to be victimized mentally, physically, and spiritually.

We have all encountered invasions of foreign substances, irritants, or disparities such as lack of similarity or equality, inequality, or difference. These and other issues have caused us countless generational internal and/or external adversities that may be difficult to overcome. These challenges have sickened many of us mentally, physically, and spiritually. As a result, we often keep them buried, allowing them to fester for years or even decades as they form into larger problems.

These problems can manifest themselves into hindrances, burdens, sickness, faithlessness, vision blockers, anger, or negative traditions that are unknowingly passed down from one generation to another. According to dictionary.com, an adversity is *"an adverse or unfavorable fortune or fate; a condition marked by misfortune, calamity, or distress: unfortunate event or circumstance."* As a safety precaution, we cover our hardships and setbacks with bandages, masking or suppressing them internally. When we do this, we are like a pearl covering the foreign invader that enters its space with nacre to repair the damage.

When oysters are invaded, they muster up an amazing environment underneath its shell that produces a beautiful pearl.

In our daily lives, that foreign substance or irritant represents adversity transforming us into our current selves – positively polishing our flaws into unique strengths. This metaphor has become the foundation for this book.

In this book, we are going to deep dive to the bottom of the ocean for our oysters. We will open the shell to retrieve our pearls. These priceless, hidden gems represent the unmasking of our hidden mental, physical, and spiritual adversities via our personal testimonials to unveil our truths. Some of our unveiling will shock, but the unmasking is part of our exodus from situations that kept us bound. With this book, you will be able to reset your priorities, allowing you to navigate your mental, physical, and spiritual wellness journey. This can help you conquer fears, achieve goals, strive for dreams, and clearly see your vision. You are not alone, and you will realize that there are others with testimonials similar to yours. We pray that each reader gains a better understanding and seek out other avenues to better treat their mental, physical, and spiritual adversities. You will learn how we "GIRLZ RUN THE WORLD IN PEARLS", by adorning them as a badge of our deliverance, exodus, strength, beauty, and empowerment.

Write any other applicable bible verses or quotes to this list:

_____

_____

_____

_____

_____

_____

_____

_____

_____

_____

_____

_____

_____

Continuation of applicable bible verses or quotes list:

_____

_____

_____

_____

_____

_____

_____

_____

_____

_____

_____

_____

_____

The Meditative Prayer

As you began to pray, reflect and meditate, read this prayer out loud then add any additional prayer requests as it relates to your unveiling:

Dear God to whom my blessings abundantly flow, give me strength, wisdom and guidance today, to absorb and create my personal testimonial in every conceivable way. Lord, help me to understand that in order for me to mentally, physically and spiritually heal from any negative traditions that I may have inherited or created, I must began by getting to the root of the negative traditions that caused my bitterness, anger, deception, prejudice, family secrets, hurt, self-hate, brokenness, abuse, illnesses, jealousy, and hateful attributes that these adversities have established in my life.

Help me to relate so that my self-reflection will allow me to integrate forgiveness, transgressions, deliverance, confessions, support, knowledge sharing, acceptance, love, conversations, humbleness, self-respect, worthiness, and validation so that I too can unveil my mask and heal. Lord make me over so that I may do your will, execute my vision, walk in my purpose so I may be a help others.

"…., be ye stedfast, unmoveable, always abounding in the work of the Lord, forasmuch as ye know that your labour is not in vain in the Lord." King James Version (KJV)

Write your own personal prayer because you are the steward of your testimonial. Only you know what you want to reveal and write in this journal, so ask God for what it is that you are seek mentally, physically and or spiritually:

_____

_____

_____

_____

_____

_____

_____

_____

_____

_____

_____

_____

_____

_____

Write your own personal prayer to God for what it is that you are seek physically:

_____

_____

_____

_____

_____

_____

_____

_____

_____

_____

_____

_____

_____

Write your own personal prayer to God for what it is that you are seek spiritually:

_____

_____

_____

_____

_____

_____

_____

_____

_____

_____

_____

_____

Understanding Mental, Physical and Spiritual Adversities

I also retrieved this information from my book "Girlz Run The World In Pearls Unveiling The Mask To Reveal Our Pearls" (pages 17-22) because is very important and need to be reiterated for the purpose of this journal. In Dr. Stephen Covey's book, *The 7 Habits of Highly Effective People*, Habit 5 says *"Seek First to Understand, Then to be Understood."* In summary this is when people form opinions based on their own experiences. You should work hard to understand the other person's perspective because both can see or hear the same thing but form two completely different viewpoints.

Before you began to begin to write your testimonials, we ask that you review the list as defined by the Lead Author along with the list of issues that can affect you mentally, physically, and spiritually. If you are afflicted by one area, the others will follow like a domino effect. Maintaining this balance is a must. All three must be in balance, if not, it could block your vision, goals and or dreams from realizing true abundance.

Mental Adversities

We should strive to be mentally well. I define mental wellness as *"the psychological well-being and a satisfactory adjustment to society and to the ordinary demands of life."* Knowledge is power, so indulging in the cognitive presence of mental health and mental instability can lead to the positive spectrum such as rebuilding relationships within your family, community, and workplace.

Mental Adversities could lead to decisions that affect the following areas in your life:

- Education
- Testimonials
- Finances
- Self-Love
- Forgiveness
- Friends
- Spouse/Partner
- Self-esteem
- Church/Place of Worship
- Employer
- Co-workers
- Old habits
- Addiction
- Self-doubt
- Materialism
- Fear of Judgement from Others
- Comparisons
- Lack of Communication
- Drama
- Fear

From this Mental Adversities List, write all the adversities that affect you:

_____

_____

_____

_____

_____

_____

_____

_____

_____

_____

_____

_____

_____

Physical Adversities

We should strive to be physically well. I define physical wellness as *"when the body works as well as it can."* Incorporating physical activities into your life will reduce your stress levels and improve your overall health.

Adversities can affect you physically in a variety of ways:

- Unhealthy Weight Gain/ Loss
- Unhealthy Dietary Habits
- Illness
- Knowledge of Methods
- Dangerous Cravings
- Unproductiveness
- Addictions
- Impatience
- Unrealistic Body Goals
- Transportation
- Abuse
- Commitment
- Time
- Finances
- Procrastination
- Mental Illness

From this Physical Adversities List, write all the adversities that affect you:

_____

_____

_____

_____

_____

_____

_____

_____

_____

_____

_____

_____

_____

Spiritual Adversities

We should strive to be spiritually well. I define spiritual wellness as *"measured by the amount of peace and harmony an individual experience on a daily basis."* By incorporating spiritual rooted activities into your daily life, it will help to maintain and uplift that spiritual connection to whom your blessings flow. Spirituality is universal and can be applied to all nationalities and faiths.

Adversities that can affect you spiritually include the following:

- Idols
- Lack of Faith
- Repentance
- Distractions
- Negative thoughts
- Misleading Information
- Spouse/Partner
- Friends
- Doubt
- Stressful Situations
- Toxic Relationships
- Environments
- Fear of Judgements From Disobeying
- Personal Morals
- Values
- Past Experiences
- Mental Illness
- Church
- Change in religion
- Confusion

From the Spiritual Adversities List, write all the adversities that affects you:

_____

_____

_____

_____

_____

_____

_____

_____

_____

_____

_____

_____

_____

Writing Your Testimonial

When you look at your list of adversities, what is your most common denominator? A common denominator is a shared trait:

Do your adversities fall under physical or sexual abuse, predisposed ailments, discrimination, bullying, religion, regional norms, etc.?

This could be the root cause, the generational curse or the swept under the rug family secret that you are supposed to take to your grave. This could be the reason or cause that you to pulls away, make you retreat, fight with others, overeat, bully others, abuse, overdrink alcohol, take un-prescribed drugs, self-hate, hate others, make you cry, or just make you mad.

Call it or them out because your life experiences are only known to God, you, and the person/s (if any) who caused them. Cry, pray, exercise, take a walk, meditate, or seek counseling (spiritual or physiological) especially if you discover that this process is causing you more mental anguish than it is intended.

Write down your common denominator adversities:

_____

_____

_____

_____

_____

_____

_____

_____

_____

_____

_____

_____

_____

It Is Your Time To Heal

Do not allow your adversities to continue to fester or incubate. You may feel like this revelation is too much to bare. Allow God to reveal the truth so that your deliverance can take place. Take some deep breaths and review this list again. Mediate about them. Add to your list if you can recall any other relevant adversities. You have now realized that these adversities could be causing you mental, physical and spiritual detriment. I have worked with other women using this writing technique and many had major breakthroughs and were prepared to walk away because of the pain that resurfaced once they revealed them. I advised them to meditate and walk into this phase slowly and in prayer.

There is a healing about to take place in your life so be prepared for the amount of energy it will take. Unveiling the mask that covers up anything can be life changing for all that are involved. There is no timeframe as to how long it will take because everyone had different circumstances to deal with. With that said, you must also understand that the longer you suppress these adversities, the irritants they caused them will continue to invade the wall of your oyster.

No matter how beautiful the pearl is, it is still hidden inside the mouth of the oyster, hidden at the bottom of the ocean. That beautiful pearl represents you and the adversities that those irritants created that you need to reveal to heal.

Write exactly how you feel at this moment (anger, hate, love hurt, excited, confused, scared, torn etc.:

_____

_____

_____

_____

_____

_____

_____

_____

_____

_____

_____

_____

_____

Your Adversities Will Lead To Your Testimonial

One way to remove your pearl from the oyster is to testify as our testimonials relates to the blessing that you encounter as well as the real-life adversities you experience in your life. The black church has been the forefront for using this method because it encourages the congregation to have faith, share of God's goodness and/or learn from other's experiences. This was a plus because we were not allowed to utilize the medical facilities as whites due to discrimination and racism. There was and still is great but not everyone was comfortable sharing adversities that caused them pain. Others simply just do not feel comfortable with public speaking. We cannot mention that the abused, raped or bullied children rarely stood in front of a congregation to testify on their life experience so they suffered in silence on into their adulthood. Are you one of them? If at any time this journal becomes unbearable seek professional help.

This journal is not a substitute for professional assistance. If you are not aware of the type of assistance you may need, I found an article written by Marie Miguel 1/21/2020 article "What's the Difference Between a Psychologist and a Psychiatrist?"

She explains that a psychologist is someone who meets with clients or patients and works through mental health or general life issues using talk therapy. A psychologist can diagnose mental health disorders, but they can't prescribe medication. On the other hand,-a psychiatrist can both diagnose and prescribe medication for these issues. A psychiatrist can also provide medication management for different diagnoses. For example, if someone has bipolar disorder and they're taking antipsychotics, a psychologist couldn't help them with medication management; they'd have to see a psychiatrist regularly. Many people see both types of providers. www.msn.com.

Your 1st Testimonial

Now that you have revealed your adversities and how they made you feel, let's began to write your 1st testimonial.

My oyster was invaded by the irritant or foreign substance of (list your common denominator/s adversities)

_____

_____.

In my testimonial I am removing my pearl from this oyster to unveil the mask of this negative tradition.

Describe the incidents only. Write in full detail exactly what happen, your age at the time, season, location, where did it occur (home, school, etc.), year, and all persons involved:

_____

_____

_____

_____

_____

_____

_____

My 1st Testimonial Continuation

_____

_____

_____

_____

_____

_____

_____

_____

_____

_____

_____

_____

_____

My 1st Testimonial Continuation

_____

_____

_____

_____

_____

_____

_____

_____

_____

_____

_____

_____

_____

My 1st Testimonial Continuation

_____

_____

_____

_____

_____

_____

_____

_____

_____

_____

_____

_____

_____

My 1st Testimonial Continuation

_____

_____

_____

_____

_____

_____

_____

_____

_____

_____

_____

_____

_____

My 1st Testimonial Continuation

_____

_____

_____

_____

_____

_____

_____

_____

_____

_____

_____

_____

_____

My 1st Testimonial Continuation

_____

_____

_____

_____

_____

_____

_____

_____

_____

_____

_____

_____

_____

My 1st Testimonial Continuation

_____

_____

_____

_____

_____

_____

_____

_____

_____

_____

_____

_____

_____

My 1st Testimonial Continuation

_____

_____

_____

_____

_____

_____

_____

_____

_____

_____

_____

_____

1st Testimonial (Mental) Summary

How did the adversities in your testimonial affect you mentally?
Did you have a mental break down, became withdrawn,
attempted suicide, feel hurt etc.?

_____

_____

_____

_____

_____

_____

_____

_____

_____

_____

_____

1ˢᵗ Testimonial (Physical) Summary

How did the adversities in your testimonial affect you physically? Did you have medical treatments, became disabled, self-medicated, pregnant, eating disorders, gain weight or became idle etc.?

_____

_____

_____

_____

_____

_____

_____

_____

_____

_____

_____

1st Testimonial (Spiritual) Summary

How did the adversities in your testimonial affect you spiritually?
Did you lose faith, feel like God abandoned you, stopped praying,
stop going to church, etc.?

_____

_____

_____

_____

_____

_____

_____

_____

_____

_____

1st Testimonial Summary Statement

As a (*write common denominator adversity*)

_____survivor,

my pearls represent the (*write the mental, physical and spiritual harm these adversities caused*)

_____

_____

 I endured because I did not and or will not allow this/these adversities to destroy my destiny. I own my mental, physical, and spiritual journey and continue to take things one day at a time with reminders to self-care and give back because God has blessed me with a testimonial to help others. Therefore, I am a girl who runs the world in my pearls as a:

_____

_____

_____

_____

_____

_____

_____

1st Testimonial Summary Statement Continued

Your 2nd Testimonial

Now that you have revealed your adversities and how they made you feel, let's began to write your testimonial.

My oyster was invaded by the irritant or foreign substance of (list your common denominator/s adversities)

_____

_____.

In my testimonial I am removing my pearl from this oyster to unveil the mask of this negative tradition.

Describe the incidents only. Write in full detail exactly what happen, your age at the time, season, location, where did it occur (home, school, etc.), year, and all persons involved:

_____

_____

_____

_____

_____

_____

_____

My 2nd Testimonial Continuation

_____

_____

_____

_____

_____

_____

_____

_____

_____

_____

_____

_____

_____

_____

My 2nd Testimonial Continuation

_____

_____

_____

_____

_____

_____

_____

_____

_____

_____

_____

_____

_____

_____

My 2nd Testimonial Continuation

_____

_____

_____

_____

_____

_____

_____

_____

_____

_____

_____

_____

_____

My 2nd Testimonial Continuation

_____

_____

_____

_____

_____

_____

_____

_____

_____

_____

_____

_____

_____

_____

My 2nd Testimonial Continuation

My 2nd Testimonial Continuation

_____

_____

_____

_____

_____

_____

_____

_____

_____

_____

_____

_____

_____

My 2nd Testimonial Continuation

_____

_____

_____

_____

_____

_____

_____

_____

_____

_____

_____

_____

_____

_____

My 2nd Testimonial Continuation

_____

_____

_____

_____

_____

_____

_____

_____

_____

_____

_____

_____

_____

2nd Testimonial (Mental) Summary

How did the adversities in your testimonial affect you mentally?
Did you have a mental break down, became withdrawn,
attempted suicide, feel hurt etc.?

_____

_____

_____

_____

_____

_____

_____

_____

_____

_____

_____

2nd **Testimonial (Physical) Summary**

How did the adversities in your testimonial affect you physically? Did you have medical treatments, became disabled, self-medicated, pregnant, eating disorders, gain weight or became idle etc.?

_____

_____

_____

_____

_____

_____

_____

_____

_____

_____

_____

_____

2nd Testimonial (Spiritual) Summary

How did the adversities in your testimonial affect you spiritually? Did you lose faith, feel like God abandoned you, stopped praying, stop going to church, etc.?

_____

_____

_____

_____

_____

_____

_____

_____

_____

_____

_____

_____

2nd **Testimonial Summary Statement**

As a (*write common denominator adversity*)

_____survivor,

my pearls represent the (*write the mental, physical and spiritual harm these adversities caused*)

_____

_____

 I endured because I did not and or will not allow this/these adversities to destroy my destiny. I own my mental, physical, and spiritual journey and continue to take things one day at a time with reminders to self-care and give back because God has blessed me with a testimonial to help others. Therefore, I am a girl who runs the world in my pearls as a:

_____

_____

_____

_____

_____

_____

_____

2nd Testimonial Summary Statement Continued

_____

_____

_____

_____

_____

_____

_____

_____

_____

_____

_____

_____

_____

Your 3rd Testimonial

Now that you have revealed your adversities and how they made you feel, let's began to write your testimonial.

My oyster was invaded by the irritant or foreign substance of (list your common denominator/s adversities)

_____

_____.

In my testimonial I am removing my pearl from this oyster to unveil the mask of this negative tradition.

Describe the incidents only. Write in full detail exactly what happen, your age at the time, season, location, where did it occur (home, school, etc.), year, and all persons involved:

_____

_____

_____

_____

_____

_____

_____

3rd My Testimonial Continuation

_____

_____

_____

_____

_____

_____

_____

_____

_____

_____

_____

_____

_____

3rd **My Testimonial Continuation**

_____

_____

_____

_____

_____

_____

_____

_____

_____

_____

_____

_____

_____

_____

3rd My Testimonial Continuation

_____

_____

_____

_____

_____

_____

_____

_____

_____

_____

_____

_____

_____

_____

3rd My Testimonial Continuation

_____

_____

_____

_____

_____

_____

_____

_____

_____

_____

_____

_____

_____

_____

3rd My Testimonial Continuation

_____

_____

_____

_____

_____

_____

_____

_____

_____

_____

_____

_____

_____

_____

3rd My Testimonial Continuation

_____

_____

_____

_____

_____

_____

_____

_____

_____

_____

_____

_____

_____

_____

3rd My Testimonial Continuation

_____

_____

_____

_____

_____

_____

_____

_____

_____

_____

_____

_____

_____

_____

3rd My Testimonial Continuation

_____

_____

_____

_____

_____

_____

_____

_____

_____

_____

_____

_____

_____

_____

3rd Testimonial (Mental) Summary

How did the adversities in your testimonial affect you mentally?
Did you have a mental break down, became withdrawn,
attempted suicide, feel hurt etc.?

_____

_____

_____

_____

_____

_____

_____

_____

_____

_____

_____

_____

3rd Testimonial (Physical) Summary

How did the adversities in your testimonial affect you physically? Did you have medical treatments, became disabled, self-medicated, pregnant, eating disorders, gain weight or became idle etc.?

_____

_____

_____

_____

_____

_____

_____

_____

_____

_____

_____

3rd Testimonial (Spiritual) Summary

How did the adversities in your testimonial affect you spiritually? Did you lose faith, feel like God abandoned you, stopped praying, stop going to church, etc.?

_____

_____

_____

_____

_____

_____

_____

_____

_____

_____

_____

3rd Testimonial Summary Statement

As a (*write common denominator adversity*)

_____survivor,

my pearls represent the (*write the mental, physical and spiritual harm these adversities caused*)

_____

_____

I endured because I did not and or will not allow this/these adversities to destroy my destiny. I own my mental, physical, and spiritual journey and continue to take things one day at a time with reminders to self-care and give back because God has blessed me with a testimonial to help others. Therefore, I am a girl who runs the world in my pearls as a:

_____

_____

_____

_____

_____

_____

_____

3rd Testimonial Summary Statement Continued

_____

_____

_____

_____

_____

_____

_____

_____

_____

_____

_____

_____

_____

Creating Your Ultimate Vision Board Experience

Habakkuk 2:2 KJV *"And the LORD answered me, and said, Write the vision, and make it plain upon tables………*

You have unveiled the mask of those adversities that kept you bound. In other words you have removed your beautiful pearl that represents your adversities from the mouth of the oyster. So wear those pearls proudly. Those adversities made you who you are. These adversities blinded, you, kept you contemplating your purpose blocked your vision, goals or dreams. You have now discovered what mental, physical and spiritual area(s) in particular you need to focus on more to keep your mind and heart clear so you can hear God. You have worked hard to create an atmosphere of positivity and sisterhood - giving you the drive to pursue your vision, goals or dreams you doubted that you could ever achieve.

It is time for you to execute your vision, goals or dreams so you can reach your fullest potential. Don't ever let others make you feel guilty because God blessed you with a gift that creates additional streams of income. It says in **3 John 1:2** KJV *"Beloved, I wish above all things that thou mayest prosper and be in health, even as thy soul prospereth."*

Wear your pearls! I chose to correlate pearls because they are to do the following:

- Be a daily reminder to encourage women to take on the world; to focus on self-care;
- Embrace the fact that their adversities are meant to define who they are;
- Use those adversities to claim individual prosperity and abundance.

They also serve as an inspiration and reminder as women walk in their journey – seeking empowerment, strength, and power. Find areas that will allow you opportunities to utilize your testimonial to help others.

As an example, my mission of mentoring others was established through my own critical experiences of learning how to set boundaries and the importance of self-care.

In the early years of my children's lives, I set lofty goals of earning three degrees in three years – during which time my now ex-husband and the father of my children was in the military overseas.

In an effort to stay true to my self-imposed deadlines, I found myself stretched in the areas of mental, physical and spiritual health. Through pushing myself past the limits, I started to develop hives. After many tests with no clear indications of any explanation for this development, a doctor inquired to the level of anxiety and stress in my life.

The impending conversation led to the realization that I needed to take immediate action in resetting my life to avoid further nerve damage, which could have ultimately led to a mental breakdown from exhaustion. After coming to this realization, I reincorporated self-care elements back into my life, I was able to finish school in a more balanced way.

The reality is that a lot of people are going through the same even in their twenties so age does not make a difference. *"People will use you until they make and then drop you or you get stuck in follower-ship."* Therefore foregoing your goals, vision and dream.

By building a legacy of support and hope through my network of like-minded women, I founded my non-profit organization Dynamic Participators. We are forging a strong path of growing the movement on a national level and touring the United States to spread of vision of hope and abundance.

Now that you are mentally, physically, and spiritually balanced, let God use you as his vessel. When you are positive then you draw positivity. When you are negative, the same applies. Have you noticed that misery really does love company? This is why it is the best time in this stage of your deliverance from adversities, to focus and execute your vision. You are now more positive, your energy is high, and you can now hear the direction that God is telling you.

I have been a participant of vision board events and have noticed that a preponderance of these classes provide supplies, food and fun but no substance. At the end of these classes we shared our boards with others. Many of the attendees added high dollar value material items to their board. They take their vision board home just to collect dust and the participant vision sits idle. They then wonder why they cannot seem to execute their goals, visions and dreams that they placed on their vision boards not realizing that there is more to it. That is why I needed to add this section to the book. Now that you understand how your adversities can keep you bound and block your vision, you will be able to use and recommend to others, this journal to write your testimonial to unmask the negative traditions.

Like me, you may not be envisioning the glitz and glam lifestyle. Let's get back to what God has placed on your heart and gifted you with, then watch the blessing flow once you execute your vision. Many visions remain idle because of adversities, but you have unveiled them, and you are now ready to create write your vision.

One way to start is to create a vision board or just keep a well-written vision in a place that is easily assessable to refer to when you need to update or add to it. I have seen it done both ways with success. The benefits of creating a vision board is that it provides you with a plan. A vision board creates an emotional connection that motivates you and makes real the dream in your mind, so you begin to believe it's possible. In other words, your faith will be a very important factor because it motivates you. A vision board can help clarify what you want out of your life. Yes, we ask God and pray for guidance, but the board is like an affirmation and keep you walking in your purpose.

I had set various goals that I wanted to achieve, including my aspiration to become a published author. In establishing my focus of desired accomplishments, I added these goals to my vision board. I didn't expect the book projects to be realized so quickly. Soon after, I was approached to become part of a book collaboration. This was concept that I wasn't familiar with, but inevitably turned out to be more fiscally attainable than writing a book solo. I am ecstatic to report that I have now coauthored five other books.

Vision Boards are all about manifesting what you want using the laws of attraction. Now that your adversities are no longer blocking your vision, your focus with confidence and profound belief in God plays a huge role in attaining the intangible and tangible things you want.

Some post their vision boards on their wall or carry their list in their purse where they can visibly see it each day. This helps to keep them motivated. Whichever way you decide, don't allow yours vision board to collect dust or expect anything to happen if you do not put forth an effort to execute them. For example, if you want to become a multi-million-dollar real estate agent, you have to gather the information, enroll in the class, then pass the exam to become certified. Be realistic: if you put a picture of a mansion on your board but you do nothing to work towards making that purchase, you will eventually lose faith in the process.

Surround yourself with people or things that relate to your vision. Join groups or organizations that can assist you in reaching your goals. We have all heard our Pastor quote *"Faith without work is dead."*

For your vision board you will need pictures that represent the people, places and things you are envisioning. Decide on the areas your vision will fulfil such as self-improvement, relationships, financial, career, or health. Give your vision a timeframe. It would behoove you to refer to the mental, physical and spiritual adversities list to add wellness elements to maintain your self-care. You can add pictures from magazines or other sources that represent your vision You can glue them on a poster board and write affirmations next to them. You can be very creative and decorate it to match your home interior if you intend to place it on your wall. Some prefer to see their board as a daily reminder.

Here is an example of my 2019 vison board.

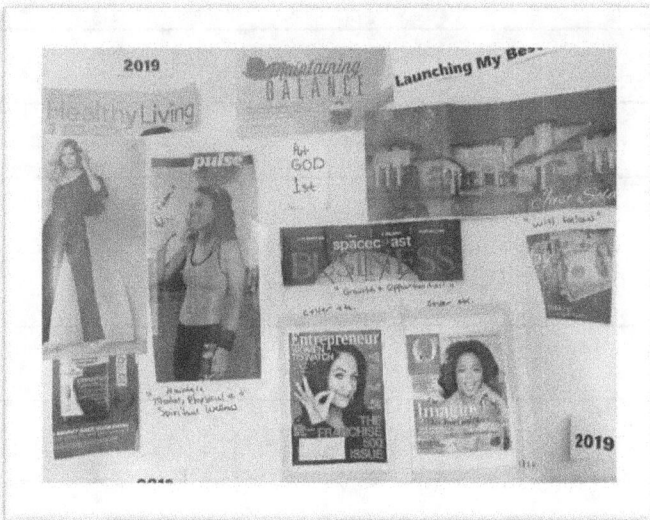

Continue to refer back to your vision board or list to ensure to keep you motivated. You can add or delete items on your board as your vision may become clearer as you execute it. Don't have tunnel vision, be prepared for your vison to grow like a tree with branches. Each branch represents a sub-vision of another.

Use this space to write your vision, goals or dreams.

_____

_____

_____

_____

_____

_____

_____

_____

_____

_____

_____

_____

Continue to write your vision, goals or dreams:

_____

_____

_____

_____

_____

_____

_____

_____

_____

_____

_____

_____

_____

_____

_____

Continue to write your vision, goals or dreams:

_____

_____

_____

_____

_____

_____

_____

_____

_____

_____

_____

_____

_____

_____

_____

Author's Closing Prayer

I come again God to whom my blessings flow. I pray for myself and the women all over the world who read this book to become more aware of our adversities that have held us back from our destinies. I pray that we get delivered from the people, place or things that won't allow us be great as you deemed us to be.

I do not speak of all material riches but those intangibles such as mental, physical and spiritual stability that is needed in order to execute our dreams and visions. Let us understand that unveiling the mask of our negative traditions is the first step, then the healing and exodus can take place. We need us women all over the world to come together to make earth as beautiful as you created it. We cannot contribute, build, or provide the strength our families, communities, churches and schools if we have none to give because our adversities are holding us back. In your name we pray, AMEN.

About the Author

Annette Watson-Johnson is a graduate of National University of California. She earned her Master of Arts in Human Resource Management. She is an Alumnus from the University of Maryland where she earned her Bachelor of Science in Business Management and an Associate of Arts in Business Administration. She also earned a Level III in Federal Acquisitions.

Annette is a President, Founder, CEO, Mentor, Wellness Ambassador, and Motivational Speaker. She has always been an advocate of wellness and is the visionary and CEO of the non-profit organization Dynamic Participators Enterprise Inc. (dP). They affirm the fact that the trilogy (Mental, Physical and Spiritual Wellness) are all correlated and must be incorporated into all aspects of our daily lives. They endorse this trilogy by these means: professional consultation, motivational workshops, retreats, social media groups, community outreach activities, virtual events, motivational material, youth mentoring activities, and symposium-style methods.

They also form partnerships with churches; profit & non-profit organizations, federal entities, community outreach projects, family reunions, local schools and districts, and all other interested parties. These techniques are not all inclusive of the variety of services they offer, because they realize that as our company continues to grow, new ideas, data and customer demands may warrant updated and innovative methodologies.

They strive to be the premier company, highly sought after to teach, promote, and encourage the incorporation of the trilogy of our services encompassing family, community, and organizational employee well-being.

As this organization flourishes Annette realized that God had more in store for her. In March of last year while she slept, she heard God speak to her. He said, *"Just Get Well"*. Not knowing what it all meant she just put it on hold and did not pursue it any further.

Annette is the Founder of AWJ Products LLC, which houses her GIRLS RUN THE WORLD IN PEARLS projects, books, and sea moss businesses.

She has been on the Amazon Best-Selling Author list four times, is a Motivational Speaker, and Wellness Ambassador. She has a plethora of knowledge in the trilogy (Mental, Physical and Spiritual Wellness) areas. Annette has had the opportunity to live and work in localities such as Okinawa, Japan; Sigonella, Sicily; Newport, Rhode Island; Gaithersburg, Maryland; San Diego, California; Tampa and Orlando, Florida. Since her high school days as an

All-American Track Star, she has remained an avid runner and love to share the health benefits of walking, running, eating choices and importance of vitamins with others.

Fast forward to 2020 when the COVID19 pandemic appeared across the world and began to affect the lives of the less healthy, she revisited this dream. Once it reached the U.S. it caused havoc in many of the black communities due to medical disparities. God blessed her to create an organic sea moss skin, hair and powder self-care product that helps build the immune system of those with health deficiencies. (These are the ones who are more susceptible to viruses.) She looks forward to what God has for her next.

She manages her online store called Girlz Run The World In Pearls. The majority of the products sold in this store are adorned in pearls. This store is part of the global movement to encourage women to self-reflect and self-care. Women should come out of their oysters to be the strong & beautiful jewels of the world. They should wear the pearls to represent as they feel more empowered to take on the world in their pearls. This is her 6th book and not her last so stay tuned.

There are a plethora of communication channels to contact Annette as listed below.

Social media handles:

Dynamic Participators Enterprise Inc.:

- Website: www.dynamicparticipators.org
- **Email:** dynamicparticipators@gmail.com
- **Instagram:** @dynamicparticipators

- **Facebook:** @dynamicparticipators
- **Twitter:** @dynamicparticipators1
- **Other:** YouTube Channel: dynamicparticipators
- **Phone:** 813-334-3120

Dynamic AWJ Products LLC

- **Website:** www.girlzruntheworldinpearls.com
- **Email:**girlzruntheworldinpearls@gmail.com
- **Instagram:** @CEO_anetjay4ever
- **Facebook:** @girlzruntheworldinpearls
- **Facebook:** @JustGetWellSeaMossProducts
- **Other:** https://www.etsy.com/shop/JustGetWellSeaMoss
- **Phone:** 813-334-3120

Need Immediate Help In A Crisis?

National Suicide Prevention Lifeline – Call 800-273-TALK (8255)
If you or someone you know is in crisis—whether they are considering suicide or not—please call the toll-free Lifeline at 800-273-TALK (8255) to speak with a trained crisis counselor 24/7.

The National Suicide Prevention Lifeline connects you with a crisis center in the Lifeline network closest to your location. Your call will be answered by a trained crisis worker who will listen empathetically and without judgment. The crisis worker will work to ensure that you feel safe and help identify options and information about mental health services in your area. Your call is confidential and free.

Crisis Text Line – Text NAMI to 741-741
Connect with a trained crisis counselor to receive free, 24/7 crisis support via text message.

National Domestic Violence Hotline – Call 800-799-SAFE (7233)
Trained expert advocates are available 24/7 to provide confidential support to anyone experiencing domestic violence or seeking resources and information. Help is available in Spanish and other languages.

National Sexual Assault Hotline – Call 800-656-HOPE (4673)
Connect with a trained staff member from a sexual assault service provider in your area that offers access to a range of free services. Crisis chat support is available at Online Hotline. Free help, 24/7.

For more information visit: **https://www.nami.org/help**

Annette Watson-Johnson
(Lead Author)

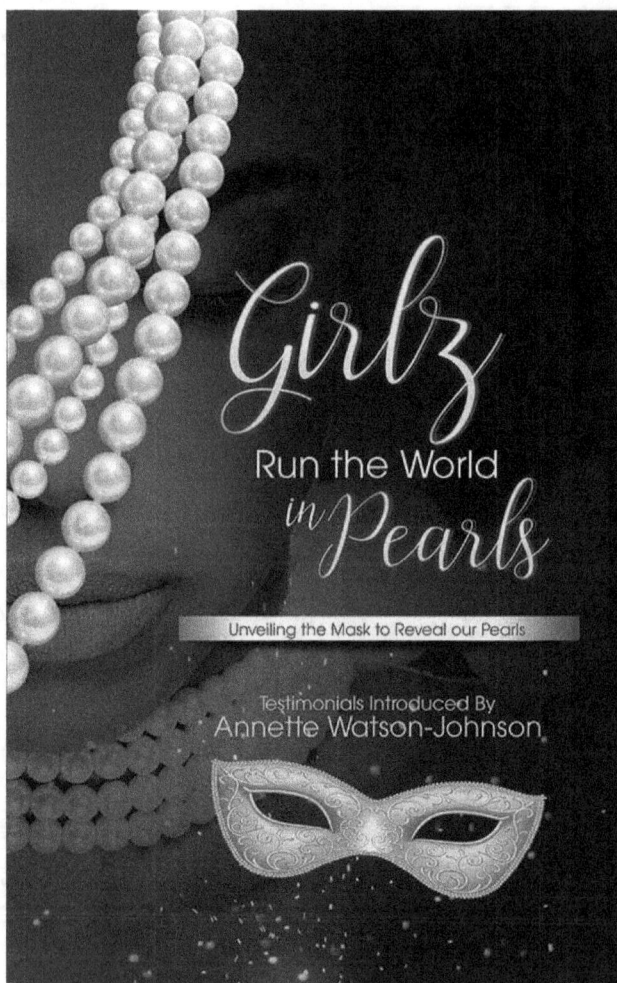

One Hundred Words of Motivation
ISBN 978-0-578-76465-8
Paper Back ~ $19.99
Kindle ~ $2.99

Also By

Annette Watson-Johnson
(Contributing Author)

One Hundred Words of Motivation
ISBN 9781733869676
Paper Back ~ $12.99
Kindle ~ $4.99

Also By

Annette Watson-Johnson
(Contributing Author)

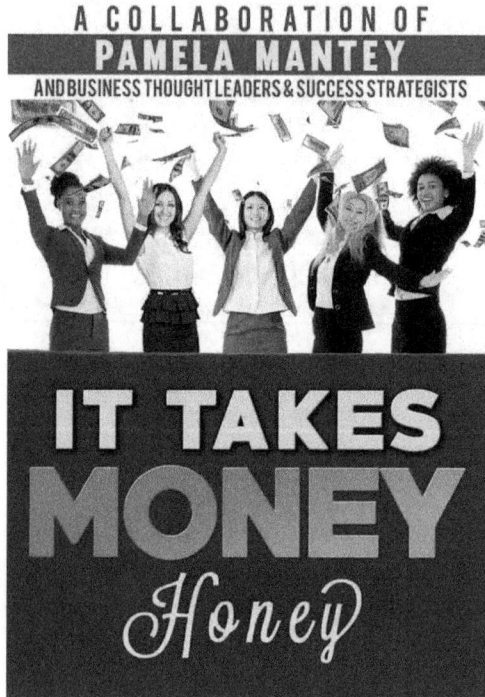

It Takes Money Honey
ISBN-13: 978-1095575499
Paper Back ~ $19.99
Kindle ~ $4.99

Also By

Annette Watson-Johnson
(Contributing Author)

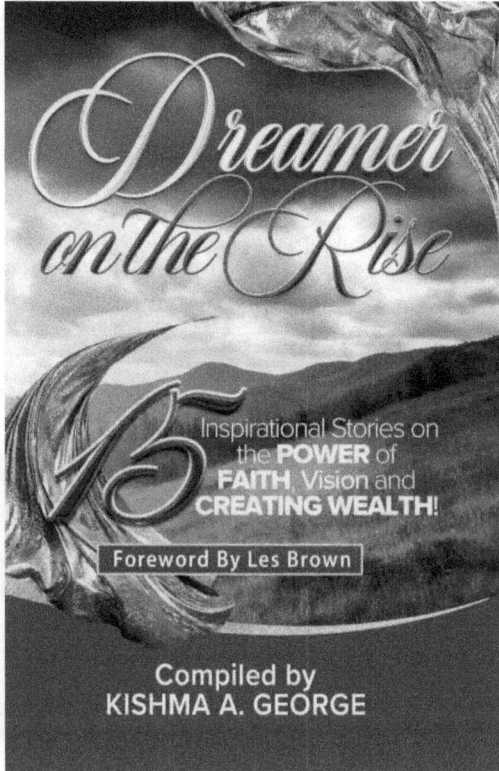

Dreamers on the Rise
ISBN-13: 978-1945377112
Paper Back ~ $19.99
Kindle ~ $4.99

To get your autographed copy of my paperback book/s
Pay Pal (cost of book plus $5.00 S&H per book)
https://www.paypal.me/AnnetteWatsonJohnson

Scan. Pay. Go.

Please list book/s you want in your order.

All Kindle orders:
amazon.com/author/annettej4ever

Made in the USA

Rockledge, FL

November 2020

$9.99
ISBN 978-0-578-78030-6
50999>

9 780578 780306

www.ingramcontent.com/pod-product-compliance
Lightning Source LLC
LaVergne TN
LVHW052036080426
835513LV00018B/2348